Meditating on Love and Mercy

Divine Mercy Devotional

Diary of St. Maria Faustina Kowalska: Divine Mercy in My Soul © 1987 Marian Fathers of the Immaculate Conception, Stockbridge, MA 01263. Used with Permission. The author of the book retains sole copyrights to her contributions to the book.

© 2011 Cynthia Alford. All rights reserved.

Art of Divine Mercy, by Tommy Canning used with permission. For a stirring and spectacular journey through Creation, to the First Great Act of Mercy, to the Triumph of the Cross and the Glory of the Saints, visit his website at www.art-of-divinemercy.co.uk. All Divine Mercy images are available on his website as well. I am truly grateful to Tommy Canning for his contribution of exquisite sacred art.

Devotional to the Divine Mercy

Novena Chaplet
with Prayers

Selected from the Diary of
St. Maria Faustina Kowalska

To the Body of Christ the Church,
and most especially the Parishioners of St. Maria Goretti Church
and the Franciscan Friars who shepherd us
teaching, promoting and responding obediently
to the Divine Mercy.

I ask every blessing from God upon this devotional booklet. May it bring souls to Christ, and redound to the sanctification of the Church, priests, bishops and the conversion of sinners.

The Divine Mercy Chaplet is a tremendous weapon in this age of spiritual warfare. To the most compassionate heart of the Divine Mercy in Your ocean of mercy and goodness we pray for an end to abortion.

Compilation

By

Cynthia L. Alford

Special thanks of gratitude to my son, Steven, for his advice on editing, layout, love and support.

Table of Contents

The Pope of Eminent Mercy: Pope John Paul II 6-7
Introduction.. 8-9

Living Witness of God's Mercy 10-12
Sacred Art - Beauty that Saves Us..13
The Image of the Divine Mercy 14

The Chaplet of the Divine Mercy 15-17
Novena to the Divine Mercy 18-25

Mercy Stations 25
St. Faustina's Praises of Divine Mercy 26-28
The Three o' Clock Hour of Mercy 29

Sin Wounds Us, the Sacrament of Reconciliation Heals Us...............................30
Aid to Examine your Conscience for a Good Confession 31-32
Our Lord Demands it: You must Perform Deeds of Mercy 33

The Eucharist 34
The Eucharist: The Banquet of Nourishment...35
A Continuous Outpouring of Love..35

Summerizing His Message of Mercy 36
Divine Mercy Sunday 37-38
You Are Not Yet Lost 39

Celebrate Divine Mercy Sunday 40-43

Selection of Prayers 44
Conversion of Sinners, St. Faustina's Prayer for Sinners 44
In Times of Suffering, To the Mother of God 45
For the Grace to be Merciful to Others 46
Memorare to St. Joseph, For a Merciful Heart, For Priests 47
For one's Country, For a Good Death, For Divine Mercy 48

The Pope of Eminent Mercy, Pope John Paul II

Throughout the life of Pope John Paul II, he consistently proclaimed and lived the teachings of divine mercy. Divine mercy was tenderly wrapped around his entire pontificate. Pope John Paul II preached and described divine mercy as the answer to the world's problems in his writings and in his homilies. He wrote an encyclical on Divine Mercy.

"*The Message of Divine Mercy has always been near and dear to me... which I took with me to the See of Peter and which it in a sense forms the image of this Pontificate.*"

One of the great events of the Jubilee 2000, with more than 200,000 people packing St. Peter's Square, the Holy Father Pope John Paul II, conducted the ceremony of the canonization of St Faustina, on April 30, 2000, not in Poland in Rome to emphasize that divine mercy is for the whole world.

"*On that same day, Pope John Paul II surprised the entire world by establishing Divine Mercy Sunday (the feast day associated with the Message of the Divine Mercy) as a feast day for the entire Church. The feast day falls on the Second Sunday of the Easter season.*"

On that day, Pope John Paul II declared, "*This is the happiest day of my life.*" "*This fulfills the Lord's request perfectly,*" he explained.

Mercy Sunday is the last day of the Octave of Easter, so it was already a part of the Feast of Easter. So, from now on, the Sunday after Easter will be known as 'Divine Mercy Sunday' just as the Lord asked in His revelations to St. Faustina."

In 2002, the Pope entrusted the whole world to Divine Mercy when he consecrated the International Shrine of the Divine Mercy in Lagiewniki, a suburb of Krakow in Poland. This is where St. Faustina's mortal remains are entombed. The saint lived in a convent nearby. The Pope himself remembers as a young man working in the Solvay Quarry, just a few meters from the present-day shrine. The Pope said he had been thinking about St. Faustina for a long time when he wrote his encyclical on Divine Mercy. Further, the Holy Father has frequently quoted from the Diary of St. Faustina and has prayed The Chaplet of The Divine Mercy at the saint's tomb.

Given all these associations to Divine Mercy and St. Faustina, is it not any wonder that Pope John Paul II died on the Vigil of Divine Mercy Sunday (the evening before the feast day), which fell that year on April 2, 2005. Additionally, it is not a surprise that the eminent mercy Pope John Paul II left us a message for Divine Mercy Sunday, which was read on the feast day by a Vatican official to the faithful in St. Peter's Square after a Mass that had been celebrated for the repose of the soul of the Pope.

Over and over again, Pope John Paul II has written and spoken about the need for us to turn to the mercy of God as the answer to the specific problems of our times. He has placed a strong and significant focus on the Divine Mercy message and devotion throughout his pontificate that will carry the Church long after his death.

He is truly the Pope of eminent mercy!

Introduction

Devotional booklets are compiled text to aid, comfort and to guide us in our spiritual growth. Simple child like prayer is pleasing to God. Devotion is one's willingness to serve God to wrap ourselves in prayer and openness to His call. Devotions keep us on the "path to heaven." They are food that feeds our souls!

Devotion literally means religious warmth, passion, and zeal. In our Catholic faith, it means pledging our goodwill and submitting to God as the source of all grace and mercy. The Divine Mercy Devotion, if properly practiced, will enrich life and devotion to God. The Lord gave us this devotion to help strengthen our love, trust and devotion for him. When we honor, him we honor each other. Our Lord speaks to St. Faustina in these words: **"Do all you possibly can for this work of My mercy. I desire that My mercy be worshipped, and I am giving mankind the last hope of salvation; this recourse to My mercy. My heart rejoices in this feast"** (Diary 998). Our main purpose for the Divine Mercy Devotion is to trust in God and the active love of neighbor. God expects us to exercise mercy through deeds, words and prayers. **"Receive mercy and go radiate this mercy to others"** (Diary 1074). Persevere and help be an integral part of spreading the message of the Divine Mercy! **"Souls who spread the honor of the Divine Mercy I shield through their entire life as a tender mother her infant, and at the hour of death I will not be a judge for them, but the merciful savior"** (Diary 1075).

Novena

The word "novena" comes from the Latin meaning "nine." It is a prayer that is offered for nine consecutive days. Novenas scripturally take their origin from the nine days of prayer before Pentecost. *After the Ascension, the apostles and disciples, in obedience to the Lord, gathered in the upper room and devoted themselves to constant prayer, together with Mary, the Mother of Jesus* (Acts 1:4-5).

The nine days of prayer can also be considered as a representation of the nine months of Jesus in the womb of Mary. Like Jesus our Head, we His Body are also to be born of Mary and the Holy Spirit. The nine days of prayer were gestation prior to the birth of the Church on Pentecost. So, a novena can be considered as a time of gestation before a new outpouring of the Holy Spirit.

Novenas are to be considered persistent prayer. Jesus exhorted us to continually ASK, SEEK, and KNOCK for what we need, and he gave us strong examples of the value of persistence in prayer — like the widow who kept pleading with the judge (Lk 18:1-8) and the man who woke his neighbor in the middle of the night to give him bread (Lk 11:5-9).

St. Faustina gives us a powerful example of persistence in prayer. Novenas were an important and regular part of her spiritual life. For her, they were times of intense and persevering prayer. While we participate in the Novena, we persevere in prayer for the whole world and prepare for Divine Mercy Sunday, the first Sunday after Easter.

The Divine Mercy Message

The ultimate message of our Lord to the Divine Mercy is how much he loves us and how very precious we are to him. We are the Lord's "Passion." He wants passionately for us to realize his mercy is far greater than our sins so we will race to his heart, trusting him and receiving his unfathomable mercy. We are called to be merciful to one another as God is to us. In our mercy we can change the world. Jesus' life was an example of forgiveness and mercy and he wants us to do the same for one another. The Lord's merciful heart is an endless abyss; he feeds us, loves us beyond comprehension and provides for our every need.

God pours his love out to us and in return we are expected to do the same for each other. In Matthew's Gospel the Lord says, "*Blessed are the merciful, for they shall obtain mercy,* (Mt 6:12-14) but "*Judgment is without mercy to one who has shown no mercy*" (Mt 5:7).

We must trust in the Lord completely. It means letting God be God. Trusting in him means even in moments of pure agony and despair, we agree with Jesus' words in the Garden, "*Not my will, but yours be done* (Lk. 22:42). When we ask, the Lord fills us with grace. Over and over in the scriptures it is written.

Throughout Blessed Faustina's Diary Jesus proclaims that we can depend upon his love. He alone is worthy of trust. "I am love and mercy itself" (Diary 1074). "Let no soul fear to draw near to Me, even though its sins be as scarlet" (Diary 699). When a soul approaches Me with trust, I fill it with such an abundance of graces that it cannot contain them within itself, but radiates them to other souls" (Diary 1074).

The Living Witness of God's Mercy

Once known as Sister Maria Faustina, Secretary of the Divine Mercy, now belongs today to the group of the most popular and well-known saints of the Church. Through her, the Lord Jesus communicated to the world the great message of God's mercy and reveals the pattern of Christian perfection based on trust in God and on the attitude of mercy toward one's neighbors.

She was born on August 25, 1905 in Glogowiec, Poland of a poor and religious family of peasants, the third of ten children. At the young age of seven, she had begun to feel her heart being "tugged" by our Lord to the religious vocation. She stood out among others because of her love of prayer, work, obedience and her sensitivity to the poor. Called during a vision of the Suffering Christ, on August 1, 1925, she entered the Congregation of the Sisters of Our Lady of Mercy and took the name Sister Maria Faustina Kowalska, her birth name Helena Kowalska.

Externally, nothing revealed her rich mystical interior life. She performed her tasks with zeal and faithfully observed the rules of religious life. She was serene and full of kindness. Although her life was apparently insignificant, monotonous and dull, she hid within herself an extraordinary union with God. It is the mystery of the mercy of God which she contemplated in the word of God as well as in the everyday activities of her life that form the basis of her spirituality. The process of contemplating and getting to know the mystery of God's mercy helped develop within St. Maria Faustina the attitude of child-like trust in God as well as mercy toward one's neighbors. *O my Jesus, each of Your saints reflects one of Your virtues; I desire to reflect Your compassionate heart, full of mercy; I want to glorify it. Let Your mercy, O Jesus, be impressed upon my heart and soul like a seal, and this will be my badge in this and the future life* (Diary 1242). Sister Faustina was a faithful daughter of the Church which she loved like a Mother, and a mystic body of Jesus Christ. Conscious of her role in the Church, she cooperated with God's mercy in the task of saving lost souls. At the specific request of and following the example of the Lord Jesus, she made a sacrifice of her own life for this very goal.

In her spiritual life, she also distinguished herself with a love of the Eucharist and a deep devotion to the Mother of Mercy. The years she had spent at the convent were filled with extraordinary gifts, such as: revelations, visions, hidden stigmata, participation in the Passion of the Lord, the gift of bilocation, the reading of human souls, the gift of prophecy, the rare gift of mystical engagement and marriage. The living relationship with God, the Blessed Mother, the angels, the saints, the souls in Purgatory — with the entire supernatural world — was as equally real for her as was the world she perceived with her senses. In spite of being so richly endowed with extraordinary graces, St. Maria Faustina knew that they do not constitute sanctity.

In the Diary of St. Faustina she wrote: *Neither graces, nor revelations, nor raptures, nor gifts granted to a soul make it perfect, but rather the intimate union of the soul with God. These gifts are merely ornaments of the soul, but constitute neither its essence nor its perfection. My sanctity and perfection consist in the close union of my will with the will of God* (Diary 1107). The Lord Jesus chose St. Maria Faustina as the Apostle and "Secretary" of His Mercy, so that she could tell the world about His great message. *In the Old Covenant,* He said to her, *"I sent prophets wielding thunderbolts to My people. Today I am sending you with My mercy to the people of the whole world. I do not want to punish aching mankind, but I desire to heal it, pressing it to My Merciful Heart"* (Diary 1588).

The mission of Saint Maria Faustina consists of three tasks:

- Reminding the world of the truth of our faith revealed in the Holy Scripture about the merciful love of God toward every human being.

- Entreating God's mercy for the whole world and particularly for sinners, among others through the practice of new forms of devotion to the Divine Mercy presented by the Lord Jesus, such as: the veneration of the image of the Divine Mercy with the inscription: *Jesus, I Trust in You,* the feast of the Divine Mercy celebrated on the first Sunday after Easter, Chaplet to the Divine Mercy and prayer at the Hour of Mercy (three o' clock). The Lord Jesus attached great promises to the above forms of devotion, provided one entrusted one's life to God and practiced active love of one's neighbor.

- Initiating the apostolic movement of the Divine Mercy which undertakes the task of proclaiming and entreating God's mercy for the world and strives for Christian perfection, following the precepts laid down by the Blessed St. Maria Faustina. The precepts in question require the faithful to display an attitude of child-like trust in God which expresses itself in fulfilling His will, as well as in the attitude of mercy toward one's neighbors. Today, this movement within the Church involves millions of people throughout the world; it comprises religious congregations, lay institutes, religious brotherhoods, associations, various communities of apostles of the Divine Mercy as well as individual people who take up the tasks which the Lord Jesus communicated to them through St. Maria Faustina.

The mission of St. Maria Faustina was recorded in her Diary which she kept at the specific request of the Lord Jesus and her confessors. In it, she recorded faithfully all of the Lord Jesus' wishes and also described the encounters between her soul and Him. *"Secretary of My most profound mystery,"* **the Lord Jesus said to Sr. Faustina,** *"know that your task is to write down everything that I make known to you about My mercy, for the benefit of those who by reading these things will be comforted in their souls and will have the courage to approach Me"* (Diary 1693).

In an extraordinary way, St. Maria Faustina's work sheds light on the mystery of the Divine Mercy. It delights not only the simple and uneducated people, but also scholars who look upon it as an additional source of theological research. The *Diary* has been translated into many languages.

Sister Maria Faustina, consumed by tuberculosis and by innumerable sufferings, died in Krakow at the age of just thirty three on October 5, 1938, with a reputation for spiritual maturity and a mystical union with God. The reputation of the holiness of her life grew as did the cult to the Divine Mercy and the graces she obtained from God through her intercession. In the years 1965-67, the investigative process into her life and heroic virtues was undertaken in Krakow and in the year 1968, the Beatification process was initiated in Rome.

The latter came to an end in December 1992. On April 18, 1993 Holy Father John Paul II raised Sister Faustina to the glory of the altars. Today, St. Maria Faustina's remains rest at the Sanctuary of the Divine Mercy in Krakow-Lagiewniki.

Sacred Art – Beauty that Saves Us

In the image, Jesus comes to us in total darkness; piercing the gloom of the dark age with his radiant light and glorious rays of mercy. We are living in a world that is bleeding and broken yet mankind still runs away from the light of the Lord into the darkness rejecting a culture of life and embracing a culture of death – abortion, euthanasia, suicide. The Good News is Jesus will not give up on us. His mercy is so marvelous. Our Savior has reached out and given us a new image of himself – reaching out to rescue us. Here is Jesus Christ the Good Shepherd, the Risen Lord seeking out his lost sheep in the darkness with rays of mercy and love embracing the entire world. He is seeking souls in the darkness and like the Lord tells St. Faustina, *"Be not afraid of Your Savior, O sinful soul. I make the first move to come to you, for I know that by yourself you are unable to lift yourself to Me"* (Diary 1485).

The Image of the Divine Mercy was given to us to penetrate our hearts more deeply than words can. The Lord inspires artist to create sacred art because it communicates more profoundly than doctrine. It awakens our souls to a deeper longing for our Lord and Savior. In our hearts, we all have this burning desire to gaze upon the Lord, to look into his kind and gentle eyes and be immersed and embraced with his love, to know he forgives us and we are blessed with him for an eternity.

Beautiful and sacred art influences souls, changes hearts and brings us closer to our Lord and Savior. Pope John Paul II said, *"The spirit is the mysterious artist of the universe."*

Truly, the secret of the Image of the Divine Mercy is the evangelization and the "touching" of souls in a way like no other. Beautiful works of sacred art stir the hidden bittersweet desire for God.

Through competent artists, we are gifted with a new and more powerful image of Christ proclaiming his love and mercy. How many souls will be consoled as they gaze upon the image of the Divine Mercy? The image that over and over again tells us just how special we are to Christ Jesus, our, Savior and how he yearns to grace us with his mercy and love. The image should be honored in every home and every Church throughout the world.

The Image of the Divine Mercy

Jesus, I trust in You!

On February 22, 1931 while St. Faustina was in her cell in the convent of the Sisters of Our Lady of Mercy, in Plock, Poland the image of the Lord Jesus was revealed to her. She saw Him clothed in an ankle-length white garment. His right hand raised in blessing; the left was touching the garment at the bosom where, from beneath the garment slightly drawn aside, two large rays were coming forth as though from His heart. Filled with love and passion He appears from the dark with radiant light. The two rays, according to John's Gospel (19:34-37) are the symbols of blood and water which signifies the graces of the Holy Spirit, "love and mercy." The image is a reminder of Jesus' death on the cross. Therefore, as we ponder the two rays, we understand the message of the image is His continuous outpouring of love.

Jesus said to St. Faustina: "Paint an image according to the pattern you see with the signature: Jesus, I Trust in You! I promise that the soul that will venerate this image will not perish. I also promise victory over [its] enemies already here on earth, especially at the hour of death." "By means of this image I shall be granting many graces to souls; so let every soul have access to it" (Diary 570). "I am offering people a vessel with which they are to keep coming for graces to the fountain of mercy." (327) I want this image to be solemnly blessed on the first Sunday after Easter; that Sunday is to be the Feast of Mercy" (Diary 49).

The Chaplet of the Divine Mercy

According to St. Faustina's Diary, on a Friday night in September 1935 she saw an Angel, the executor of divine wrath. He was dressed in an elegant robe, his face was glorious. When she saw the sign of the divine wrath about to strike the earth, she began to pray but her prayers were powerless. In her plea to God for mercy she seen the Most Holy Trinity and then our Lord inspired her to pray: *"Eternal Father, I offer You the Body and Blood, Soul and Divinity of Your dearly beloved Son, our Lord Jesus Christ for our sins and those of the whole world; for the sake of His sorrowful Passion, have mercy on us and on the whole world"* (Diary 475). As she prayed, the angel of divine wrath became helpless and unable to deliver the deserved punishment to the world.

The next morning in the chapel she heard the Lord say, "Every time you enter the chapel, immediately recite the prayer which I taught you yesterday" (Diary 475). As St. Faustina said the prayer she heard these words: "This prayer will serve to appease My wrath. You will recite it for nine days, on the beads of the rosary in the following manner: First of all, you will say one OUR FATHER, and HAIL MARY and the I BELIEVE IN GOD. Then on the OUR FATHER beads, you will say the following words: Eternal Father, I offer You the Body and Blood, Soul and Divinity of Your dearly beloved Son, Our Lord Jesus Christ, in atonement for our sins and those of the whole world. On the HAIL MARY beads you will say the following words: For the sake of His sorrowful Passion have mercy on us and on the whole world. In conclusion, three times you will recite these words: Holy God, Holy Mighty One, Holy Immortal One, have mercy on us and on the whole world" (Diary 476).

This chaplet is powerful and extraordinary promises are attached to it. It is one of the most principle elements of the Divine Mercy Devotional. It is appropriate and should be prayed every day at the three o' clock hour but most especially at the three o' clock hour on Divine Mercy Sunday. The Lord specifically told St. Faustina to recite it during the nine days before the Feast of Divine Mercy Sunday and added: "By this Novena, [of Chaplets] I will grant every possible grace to souls" (Diary 796). The Lord's promise: "The souls that say this chaplet will be embraced by My mercy during their lifetime and especially at the hour of death" (Diary 754). "Even if there were a sinner most hardened, if he were to recite this Chaplet only once, he would receive grace from My infinite mercy" (Diary 687).

Chaplet of the Divine Mercy

(Recite the Chaplet on ordinary rosary beads.) (Diary 476)

The Our Father
Our Father, who art in heaven, hallowed be Thy name; Thy kingdom come; Thy will be done on earth as it is in heaven. Give us this day our daily bread; and forgive us our trespasses as we forgive those who trespass against us; and lead us not into temptation, but deliver us from evil. Amen.

The Hail Mary
Hail Mary, full of grace. The Lord is with thee. Blessed art thou among women and blessed is the fruit of thy womb Jesus. Holy Mary, Mother of God, pray for us sinners, now and at the hour of our death. Amen.

The Apostles' Creed
[The text of the Apostles' Creed is an officially approved translation: see Holy Saturday Liturgy in the Roman Missal.]

I believe in God, the Father almighty, creator of heaven and earth.
I believe in Jesus Christ, His only son, our Lord. He was conceived by the power of the Holy Spirit and born of the Virgin Mary. He suffered under Pontius Pilate, was crucified, died and was buried. He descended to the dead. On the third day He rose again. He ascended into heaven, and is seated at the right hand of the Father. He will come again to judge the living and the dead.

I believe in the Holy Spirit, the holy Catholic Church, the communion of saints, the forgiveness of sins, the resurrection of the body, and life everlasting. Amen.

On the large beads before each decade:

> Eternal Father,
> I offer you
> the Body and Blood,
> Soul and Divinity
> of Your dearly beloved Son.
> Our Lord Jesus Christ,
> in atonement for our sins
> and those of the whole world.

On the small beads of each decade:

> For the sake of His sorrowful Passion,
> have mercy on us
> and on the whole world.

Concluding Doxology:
(after five decades)

> Holy God,
> Holy Mighty One,
> Holy Immortal One,
> have mercy on us
> and on the whole world.
> (Pray this three times.)

Concluding Prayer:
(optional)

Eternal God,
in whom mercy is endless and the treasury of compassion inexhaustible,
look kindly upon us and increase Your mercy in us,
that in difficult moments we might not despair nor become despondent,
but with great confidence submit ourselves to your Holy Will,
which is Love and Mercy itself.

Novena to the Divine Mercy

[It is exceptionally recommended that the Novena intentions and prayers be said together with the Chaplet of the Divine Mercy, since our Lord specifically asked for a novena of chaplets, most especially before the Feast of Mercy, Divine Mercy Sunday] (Diary 1209-1229). The Novena is prayed in celebration of Divine Mercy Sunday and begins nine days prior to Divine Mercy Sunday (Good Friday). We pray the Novena for the needs of the entire world, not for our own personal intentions.

On Good Friday, Jesus requested St. Faustina make a special novena before the Feast of Mercy, from Good Friday until the following Saturday. He himself dictated the intentions for each day to St. Faustina. By each special prayer, St. Faustina was to bring to His heart a different group of souls each day and immerse them in his ocean of mercy, begging the Father, on the strength of Jesus' Passion for grace for them (Diary 1209).

First Day

TODAY BRING TO ME, ALL OF MANKIND, ESPECIALLY ALL SINNERS, AND IMMERSE THEM IN THE OCEAN OF MY MERCY.
In this way you will console Me in the bitter grief into which the loss of souls plunges Me.

Most Merciful Jesus, whose very nature it is to have compassion on us and to forgive us, do not look upon our sins but upon our trust which we place in Your infinite goodness. Receive us all into the abode of your Most Compassionate Heart, and never let us escape from it. We beg this of You by Your love which unites You to the Father and the Holy Spirit.

Eternal Father, turn Your merciful gaze upon all mankind and especially upon poor sinners, all enfolded in the Most Compassionate Heart of Jesus. For the sake of His sorrowful Passion show us Your Mercy, that we may praise the omnipotence of Your mercy forever and ever. Amen.

Second Day

TODAY BRING TO ME, THE SOULS OF PRIESTS AND RELIGIOUS, AND IMMERSE THEM IN MY UNFATHOMABLE MERCY. It was they who gave Me strength to endure My bitter Passion. Through them as through channels My mercy flows out upon mankind.

Most Merciful Jesus, from whom comes all that is good, increase Your grace in men and women consecrated to Your service, that they may perform worthy works of mercy; and that all who see them may glorify the Father of Mercy who is in heaven.

Eternal Father, turn Your merciful gaze upon the company of chosen ones in Your vineyard upon the souls of priests and religious; and endow them with the strength of Your blessing. For the love of the Heart of your Son in which they are enfolded, impart to them Your power and light, that they may be able to guide others in the way of salvation and with one voice sing praise to Your boundless mercy for ages without end. Amen.

Third Day

TODAY BRING TO ME, ALL DEVOUT AND FATIHFUL SOULS, AND IMMERSE THEM IN THE OCEAN OF MY MERCY. These souls brought Me consolation on the Way of the Cross. They were that drop of consolation in the midst of an ocean of bitterness.

Most merciful Jesus, from the treasure of Your Mercy, You impart Your graces in great abundance to each and all. Receive us into the abode of Your Most Compassionate Heart and never let us escape from it. We beg this grace of You by that most wondrous love for the heavenly Father with which Your Heart burns so fiercely.

Eternal Father, turn Your merciful gaze upon faithful souls, as upon the inheritance of Your Son. For the sake of His sorrowful Passion, grant them Your blessing and surround them with Your constant protection. Thus may they never fail in love or lose the treasure of the Holy faith, but rather, with all the host of angels and Saints, may they glorify Your boundless mercy for endless ages. Amen.

Fourth Day

TODAY BRING TO ME, THOSE WHO DO NOT BELIEVE IN GOD AND THOSE WHO DO NOT YET KNOW ME. I was thinking also of them during My bitter Passion, and their future zeal comforted My Heart. Immerse them in the ocean of My Mercy.

Most compassionate Jesus, You are the Light of the whole world. Receive into the abode of Your Most Compassionate Heart the souls of those who do not believe in God and of those who as yet do not know You. Let the rays of Your grace enlighten them that they, too, together with us, may extol Your wonderful mercy; and do not let them escape from the abode which is Your Most Compassionate Heart.

Eternal Father, turn Your merciful gaze upon the souls of those who do not believe in You, and of those who as yet do not know You, but who are enclosed in the Most Compassionate Heart of Jesus. Draw them to the Light of the Gospel. These souls do not know what great happiness it is to love You. Grant that they, too, may extol the generosity of Your mercy for endless ages. Amen.

Fifth Day

TODAY BRING TO ME, THE SOULS WHO HAVE SEPARATED THEMSELVES FROM MY CHURCH, AND IMMERSE THEM IN THE OCEAN OF MY MERCY. During my bitter passion, they tore at My Body and Heart, that is, My Church. As they return to unity with the Church My wounds heal and in this way they alleviate My Passion.

Most Merciful Jesus, Goodness Itself. You do not refuse light to those who seek it of You. Receive into the abode of Your Most Compassionate Heart the souls of those who have separated themselves from Your Church. Draw them by Your light into the unity of the Church, and do not let them escape from the abode of Your Most Compassionate Heart; but bring it about that they, too, come to glorify the generosity of Your Mercy.

      Eternal Father, turn Your merciful gaze upon the souls of those who have separated themselves from Your Son's Church, who have squandered Your blessings and misused your graces by obstinately persisting in their errors. Do not look upon their errors, but upon the love of Your own Son and upon His bitter Passion, which He underwent for their sake, since they, too, are enclosed in His Most Compassionate Heart. Bring it about that they also may glorify Your great mercy for endless ages. Amen.

[In the Diary, our Lord used the words "heretics and schismatics," since he spoke to St. Faustina in the context of her times. As of the Second Vatican Council, Church authorities have seen fit not to use those designations in accordance with the explanation given in the Council's Decree on Ecumenism (n.3). Every pope since the Council has reaffirmed that usage. St. Faustina herself, her heart always in harmony with the mind of the Church, most certainly would have agreed.

One time, because of the decisions of her superiors and father confessor, she was not able to execute Our Lord's inspirations and orders, she declared: **"I will follow Your Will insofar as You will permit me to do so through Your representative. O my Jesus, I give priority to the voice of the Church over the voice with which You speak to me"** (Diary 497).

Sixth Day

TODAY BRING TO ME, THE MEEK AND HUMBLE SOULS AND THE SOULS OF LITTLE CHILDREN, AND IMMERSE THEM IN MY MERCY. These souls most closely resemble My Heart. They strengthened Me during My bitter agony. I saw them as earthly Angels, who will keep vigil at My Altars. I pour out upon them whole torrents of grace. Only the humble soul is capable of receiving My grace. I favor humble souls with My confidence.

Most Merciful Jesus, You yourself have said, "Learn from Me for I am meek and humble of heart." Receive into the abode of Your Most Compassionate Heart all meek and humble souls and the souls of little children. These souls send all heaven into ecstasy and they are the heavenly Father's favorites.

They are sweet-smelling bouquet before the throne of God; God Himself takes delight in their fragrance. These souls have a permanent abode in Your Most Compassionate Heart, O Jesus, and they unceasingly sing out a hymn of love and mercy.

Eternal Father, turn Your merciful gaze upon meek souls, upon humble souls, and upon little children who are enfolded in the abode which is the Most Compassionate Heart of Jesus. These souls bear the closest resemblance to Your Son. Their fragrance arises from the earth and reaches Your very throne. Father of Mercy and of all goodness, I beg You by the love You bear these souls and by the delight You take in them; Bless the whole world, that all souls together may sing out the praises of Your mercy for endless ages. Amen.

[The text leads one to make the decision that the first prayer directed to Jesus, who is the Redeemer, it is "victims" souls and contemplatives that are being prayed for; those persons, that is, that voluntarily offered themselves to God for the salvation of their neighbor (Col 1:24; Col 4:12). This explains their close union with the Savior and the extraordinary efficacy that their invisible activity has for others. In the second prayer, directed to the Father from whom comes "every worth-while gift and every genuine benefit," we recommend the "active" souls, who promote devotion to the Divine Mercy and exercise with it all other works that lend themselves to the spiritual and material uplifting their brethren.]

Seventh Day

TODAY BRING TO ME, THE SOULS WHO ESPECIALLY VENERATE AND GLORIFY MY MERCY, AND IMMERSE THEM IN MY MERCY. These souls sorrowed most over My Passion and entered most deeply into My Spirit. They are living images of My Compassionate Heart. These souls will shine with a special brightness in the next life. Not one of them will go into the fire of hell. I shall particularly defend each of them at the hour of death.

Most Merciful Jesus, Whose Heart is Love Itself, receive into the abode of Your Most Compassionate Heart the souls of those who particularly extol and venerate the greatness of Your mercy. These souls are mighty with the very power of God Himself. In the midst of all afflictions and adversities they go forward, confident of Your mercy; and united to You, O Jesus, they carry all mankind on their shoulders. These souls will be judged severely, but Your mercy will embrace them as they depart this life.

      Eternal Father, turn Your merciful gaze upon the souls who glorify and venerate Your greatest attribute, that of Your fathomless mercy, and who are enclosed in the Most Compassionate Heart of Jesus. These souls are a living Gospel; their hands are full of deeds of mercy, and their hearts, overflowing with joy, sing a canticle of mercy to You, O Most High! I beg of You O God; show them Your mercy according to the hope and trust they have placed in You. Let there be accomplished in them the promise of Jesus, who said to them that during their life, but especially at the hour of death, the souls who will venerate this fathomless mercy of His, He, Himself, will defend as His glory. Amen.

Eighth Day

TODAY BRING TO ME, THE SOULS WHO ARE DETAINED IN PURGATORY, AND IMMERSE THEM IN THE ABYSS OF MY MERCY.

      Let the torrents of My Blood cool down their scorching flames. All these souls are greatly loved by Me. They are making retribution to My justice. It is in your power to bring them relief. Draw all the indulgences from the treasury of My Church and offer them on their behalf. Oh, if you only knew the torments they suffer, you would continually offer for them the alms of the spirit and pay off their debt to My justice.

Most Merciful Jesus, You Yourself have said that You desire mercy; so I bring into the abode of Your Compassionate Heart, the souls in Purgatory, souls who are very dear to You, and yet, who must make retribution to Your justice. May the streams of Blood and Water which gushed forth from Your Heart put out the flames of Purgatory, that there, too, the power of Your mercy may be celebrated.

Eternal Father, turn Your merciful gaze upon the souls suffering in Purgatory, who are enfolded in the Most Compassionate Heart of Jesus. I beg You, by the sorrowful Passion of Jesus Your Son, and by all the bitterness with which His most sacred Soul was flooded; manifest Your mercy to the souls who are under Your just scrutiny. Look upon them in no other way but only through the Wounds of Jesus, Your dearly beloved Son; for we firmly believe that there is no limit to Your goodness and compassion. Amen.

<u>Ninth Day</u>

TODAY BRING TO ME, SOULS WHO HAVE BECOME LUKE WARM, AND IMMERSE THEM IN THE ABYSS OF MY MERCY.

These souls wound My Heart most painfully; My soul suffered the most dreadful loathing in the Garden of Olives because of lukewarm souls. They were the reason I cried out "Father, take this cup away from Me if it be Your will." For them the last hope of salvation is to run to My mercy.

Most compassionate Jesus, You are Compassion Itself. I bring lukewarm souls into the abode of Your Most Compassionate Heart. In this fire of your pure love let these tepid souls, who, like corpses, filled You with such deep loathing, be once again set aflame. O' Most Compassionate Jesus, exercise the omnipotence of Your mercy and draw them into the very ardor of Your love, and bestow upon them the gift of holy love, for nothing is beyond Your power.

Eternal Father, turn Your merciful gaze upon lukewarm souls who are nonetheless enfolded in the Most Compassionate Heart of Jesus. Father of Mercy, I beg you by the bitter Passion of Your Son and by His three-hour agony on the Cross; let them too, glorify the abyss of Your mercy. Amen. [To understand who the souls are designated for this day and who the Diary called lukewarm, and also referred to them as ice and as corpses we should refer to what our Savior Himself said to St. Faustina about them:

"There are souls who thwart My efforts (Diary 1682). " Souls without love or devotion, souls full of egoism and selfishness, proud and arrogant souls full of deceit and hypocrisy, lukewarm souls who have just enough warmth to keep themselves alive; My Heart cannot bear this. All the graces that I pour out upon them flow off them as off the face of a rock. I cannot stand them because they are neither good nor bad" (Diary 1702)].

Mercy Stations

(Try to include the Stations with the Chaplet.) Begin each station with:
Eternal Father, I offer You the Body and Blood, Soul and Divinity of Your dearly beloved Son, Our Lord Jesus Christ, in atonement for our sins and those of the whole world.

Pause briefly mediating on the Passion of Jesus. Then, say the invocation given below, followed by:

Have mercy on us and on the whole world.

Invocations

1. For the sake of His institution of the Eucharist as the memorial of His passion...
2. For the sake of His agony in the Garden...
3. For the sake of His being scourged and crowned with thorns...
4. For the sake of His being condemned to death...
5. For the sake of His carrying the Cross...
6. For the sake of His falling under the weight of the Cross...
7. For the sake of His meeting His afflicted Mother...
8. For the sake of His accepting help in carrying the Cross...
9. For the sake of His receiving mercy from Veronica...
10. For the sake of His consoling the women...
11. For the sake of His being stripped...
12. For the sake of His being crucified...
13. For the sake of His death on the Cross...
14. For the sake of His being buried...
15. For the sake of His being raised from the dead...

Holy God, Holy Mighty One, Holy Immortal One, Have mercy on us and on the whole world. *(Recite this three times.)*

St. Faustina's Praises of the Divine Mercy
(948-949)

The Love of God is the flower, mercy is the fruit.

Let the doubting soul read these considerations on Divine Mercy and become trusting.

Divine Mercy, gushing forth from the bosom of the Father,
> I trust in You.

Divine Mercy, greatest attribute of God,
> I trust in You.

Divine Mercy, incomprehensible mystery,
> I trust in You.

Divine Mercy, fountain gushing forth from the mystery of the Most blessed Trinity,
> I trust in You.

Divine Mercy, unfathomed by any intellect, human or angelic,
> I trust in You.

Divine Mercy, from which wells forth all life and happiness,
> I trust in You.

Divine Mercy, better than the heavens,
> I trust in You.

Divine Mercy, source of miracles and wonders,
> I trust in You.

Divine Mercy, encompassing the whole universe,
> I trust in You.

Divine Mercy, descending to earth in the Person of the Incarnate Word,
> I trust in You.

Divine Mercy, which flowed out from the open wound of the Heart of Jesus,
> I trust in You.

Divine Mercy, enclosed in the Heart of Jesus for us, and especially for sinners,
> I trust in You.

Divine Mercy, unfathomed in the institution of the Sacred Heart,
> I trust in You.

Divine Mercy, in the founding of Holy Church,
> I trust in You.

Divine Mercy, in the Sacrament of Holy Baptism,
> I trust in You.

Divine Mercy, in our justification through Jesus Christ,
> I trust in You.

Divine Mercy, accompanying us through our whole life,
> I trust in You.

Divine Mercy, embracing us especially at the hour of death,
> I trust in You.

Divine Mercy, endowing us with immortal life,
> I trust in You.

Divine Mercy, accompanying us every moment of our life,
> I trust in You.

Divine Mercy, shielding us from the fire of hell,
> I trust in You.

Divine Mercy, in the conversion of hardened sinners,
> I trust in You.

Divine Mercy, astonishment for Angels, incomprehensible to Saints,
> I trust in You.

Divine Mercy, unfathomable in all the mysteries of God,
> I trust in You.

Divine Mercy, lifting us out of every misery,
> I trust in You.

Divine Mercy, source of our happiness and joy,
> I trust in You.

Divine Mercy, in calling us forth from nothingness to existence,
> I trust in You.

Divine Mercy, crown of all of God's handiwork,
> I trust in You.

Divine Mercy, in which we are all immersed,
> I trust in You.

Divine Mercy, only hope of despairing souls,
> I trust in You.

Divine Mercy, repose of hearts, peace amidst fear,
> I trust in You.

Divine Mercy, delight and ecstasy of holy souls,
> I trust in You.

Divine Mercy, inspiring hope against all hope,
> I trust in You.

Eternal God, in whom mercy is endless and the treasury of compassion inexhaustible, look kindly upon us and increase Your mercy in us, that in difficult moments we might not despair nor become despondent, but with great confidence submit ourselves to Your Holy Will, which is Love and mercy itself (Diary 950).

The Three O' Clock Hour of Mercy

Our Lord requested special prayers and meditation on his passion every day at the three o' clock hour. Three o'clock is the hour of our Lord's death on the cross. **"I remind you, My daughter, that as often as you hear the clock strike the third hour, immerse yourself completely in My mercy, adoring and glorifying it; invoke its omnipotence for the whole world, and particularly for poor sinners; for at that moment mercy was opened wide for every soul. In this hour you can obtain everything for yourself and for others for the asking; it was the hour of grace for the whole world - mercy triumphed over justice"** (Diary 1572).

From these words, it is clear that our Lord wants us to think about his Passion at the three o' clock hour. We may not always be able to go and embrace the Stations of the Cross meditating on his Passion, but we can pause briefly and at least say the short prayer, "Jesus for the sake of Your sorrowful Passion, have mercy on us and on the whole world."

Sin Wounds Us, the Sacrament of Reconciliation Heals Us

Sin will always disrupt relationships. With sin there is no such thing as "it did not hurt anyone else." Mortal sins are actions that we think about, that we know are serious and do anyway, and that ruptures our relationship with God and with our community (the Body of Christ the Church). While venial sins are lesser offenses, such as to not tell the truth, to gossip or to cheat on a test or in a game, may not totally break our relationships with God and the Church community; often they wound or weaken relationships. Reconciliation requires us to reflect and to scrutinize. We seek out our sins, we capture them, call them by name. There is a Chinese saying, "The beginning of wisdom is to call something by its correct name." We name what we are: proud, greedy, lustful, petty selfish, untruthful, unkind. In reconciliation and prayer, we do this and strive to change our lives to be better.

Reconciliation means to resolve, to reunite, to bring together and to restore our oneness with God and others. We enter the world with original sin, baptism cleanses us from sin and restores the union of life that is shared in Jesus Christ. However, because we are created in God's image with the gift of freedom, we do at times freely choose to turn away from God, others and sometimes our own selves. We sin. Prepare yourself and make a good confession prior to the Feast of Divine Mercy. The parable of the prodigal son and merciful father is a story of reconciliation and coming together that mirrors God the Father's willingness to welcome us back into full relationship with Him. Passing through reconciliation with God allows us to LIVE again. Each time we emerge from the confessional, we breathe "new" again. We can see the light of hope. We are given our Lord's grace. The sacrament of reconciliation gives us a "fresh" start. Harmony is restored!

"I want to grant a complete pardon to the souls that will go to Confession and receive Holy Communion on the Feast of My Mercy" (Diary 1109). We give a whole hearted confession holding nothing back from our Lord. We promise, by the sacrament of reconciliation, to focus on God's mercy, which is love. The Gospel on Divine Mercy Sunday (John 20:19-31) is where Christ institutes the sacrament of reconciliation to the Apostles and which our Lord calls the "Fountain of Mercy" (Diary 1602). **"It is in the confessionals that the greatest miracles take place and are incessantly repeated"** (Diary 1448).

Aid to Examine your Conscience for a Good Confession

Work towards rebirth, renewal and radiance of soul. Come and engage in the "flowering" of the soul, confession!

[Sins of Commission]
1. *I am the Lord your God; you shall have no other Gods before me.*
Did I fail to love God; to make God first in my life? Do I seek his presence and pray daily? Have I doubted or denied my faith? Do I seek to love God with all my heart and with all my strength?
2. **You shall not take the Lord Your God's Name in vain.**
Did I use God's name in vain, carelessly, by blasphemy? Did I break an oath or vow?
3. **Remember to Keep Holy the Sabbath Day.**
Have I deliberately missed Mass on Sunday, Holy Days of Obligation? Did I arrive late to Mass? Did I leave Mass early?
4. **Honor your father and your mother.**
Have I loved, respected, and obeyed my parents who gave me Life? Do I care for them when they are in need or in old age? In difficulties, am I patient with them? Did I fail to spend time with my family?
5. **You shall not kill.**
Did I give in to feelings of anger or jealousy? Have I loved my neighbor, or have I physically harmed or hastened the death of another through violence, abortion, euthanasia, drugs or hatred?
6. **You shall not commit adultery.**
Have I been pure and holy in thoughts, words and actions or have I been unfaithful to my spouse or desirous of another? Have I been sexually active outside of marriage, or with another of the same sex? Have I indulged in pornography, masturbation, contraception? Did I deliberately look at impure material, television or internet?
7. **You shall not steal; you shall not covet they neighbor's goods.**
Do I respect other's goods or have I been envious and greedy, even taking what belongs to another? Have I paid my debts? Have I wasted time at work or school?
8. **You shall not bear false witness against your neighbor.**
Have I been honest, or have I lied, gossiped, given false testimony, ruined the good name of another, broken confidentiality, or denied the truth out of pride or hypocrisy?

9. **You shall not covet your neighbors' wife.** Did I neglect to control my imagination or desire other people?

10. **You shall not covet your neighbors' goods.** Is my heart greedy? Am I jealous of what others have? Is my heart set on earthly possessions?

[Sins of Omission]
- Omitting to love one another as Jesus has loved us (Jn. 15:12).
- Omitting to be merciful as the Father is merciful (Lk. 6:36).
- Omitting to forgive another as we are forgiven (Mt. 6:14-15).

[Sins of Waste]

- Waste of talents
- Waste of graces
- Waste of suffering
  God chose suffering for his Son to bring forgiveness and mercy to us all. God asked us to make use of suffering, uniting it with Christ's suffering (Phil. 1:29, Col 1:24, Lk. 9:23).

[Sins of Idolatry]
- Making idols of possessions
- Making idols of success
- Making idols of reputation

The Seven Deadly Sins:
Pride, greed, envy, lust, sloth, anger, gluttony

Act of Contrition
O my God, I am heartily sorry for having offended You,
and I detest all my sins, because I dread the loss of heaven and the pains of hell;
but most of all, because they offend You, my God, who are all good and deserving of all my love.
I firmly resolve, with the help of Your grace, to confess my sins, to do penance, and to avoid the near occasion of sin.
✝ *Jesus Christ, Son of God, have mercy on me a sinner.*

Our Lord Demands it: You must Perform Deeds of Mercy
Be merciful, even as your Father is merciful." (Lk 6:36).

"I demand from you deeds of mercy which are to arise out of love for Me. You are to show mercy to your neighbors always and everywhere. You must not shrink from this or try to excuse or absolve yourself from it. The Lord assures us that we can do this always, "When a soul approaches Me with trust," He says, "I fill it with such an abundance of graces that it cannot contain them within itself, but radiates them to other souls" (Diary 1074). Manifest God's mercy to others, by actions, words and prayers.

The Corporal Works of Mercy

1. Feed the hungry.
2. Give drink to the thirsty.
3. Clothe the naked.
4. Shelter the homeless.
5. Comfort the imprisoned.
6. Visit the sick.
7. Bury the dead.

The Spiritual Works of Mercy

1. Admonish sinners.
2. Instruct the uninformed.
3. Counsel the doubtful.
4. Comfort the sorrowful.
5. Be patient with those in error.
6. Forgive offenses.
7. Pray for the living and the dead.

The Eucharist: The Banquet of Nourishment

If we invite our Lord into our hearts, he will live in us. "*He who eats my flesh abides in me and I in Him*." (John 6:55,56) When we receive Holy Communion we are to become like Christ. It transforms us. St. Paul said, "It is no longer I who live, but Christ who lives within me." We receive him and then go out into the world with zeal to teach and evangelize, transmitting Christ love in us to others.

The Eucharist is the fountain of celestial gifts and graces. Our Lord spoke to St. Faustina: **"My great delight is to unite Myself with souls...when I come to a human heart in Holy Communion, My hands are full of all kinds of graces which I want to give to the souls** (Diary 1385).

St. Faustina was devoted to the Eucharist. She wrote, "*All the good that is in me is due to Holy Communion* (Diary 1392). *One thing alone sustains me and that is Holy Communion. From it I draw all my strength; in it is all my comfort. Jesus concealed in the Host is everything to me. I would not know how to give glory to God if I did not have the Eucharist in my hear*t (Diary 1037).

A Continuous Outpouring of Love

Each time we receive Holy Communion, we literally receive the gift of "Jesus" Body and Blood, Soul and Divinity. We have true life with Jesus in intimate communion with God. The sacrament of Holy Communion has the power to transform human interaction. Jesus said, "*If you feed on my Body and Blood, you will live forever*."

In order that we might receive every grace, Jesus reveals to St. Faustina in the Diary on Divine Mercy Sunday we must be sure to make a good confession so that we can receive the VERY BEST Holy Communion possible. The Eucharist separates us from sin. We are formed, molded, transformed each and every time we receive Christ. Christ offers himself completely and we offer ourselves completely to Christ in the intimate relationship of the Eucharist.

The Eucharist is our nutrition, our food for our souls sustaining us in our journey on earth until we reach our final destination, heaven. Each time we receive Christ we are united to the Church, intimately joined with each other - the entire Body of the Church on earth, in heaven and in purgatory.

Summarizing His Message of Mercy

The message of Mercy is that God loves us and wants us to recognize that His mercy is infinite. He wants us to trust him and to love one another. We can remember this message by these simple summaries of the ABC's of Mercy.

The ABCs of Mercy

"A" Ask for His Mercy. God wants us to approach Him in prayer constantly, repenting for our sins and asking Him to pour out His mercy upon us and the whole world.

"B" Be merciful. God wants us to receive His mercy and then to let it radiate to others. He wants us to love and to forgive each other just as He does for us.

"C" Completely trust. God wants us to know that the graces of His mercy are dependent upon our trust in Him. The more we trust the more we receive.

Through the passion of our Lord Jesus, mercy from God is infinite. We must ask. *"Ask and it will be given to you...for everyone who asks, receives"* (Mt. 7:7,8).

Pope John Paul II proclaimed a Scriptural message with urgency for our times, *"At no time, especially at a moment as critical as our own can the Church forget the prayer that is a cry for the mercy of God. The Church has the right and the duty to appeal to the God of Mercy with loud cries"* (Rich in Mercy, 15).

Through St. Faustina, we have been given three new ways to ask for our Lord's mercy: the Novena, including the chaplet, prayer and adoration at the three o' clock hour. **"Souls that make an appeal to My mercy delight Me. To such souls I grant even more than they ask. I cannot punish even the greatest sinner if he makes an appeal to My compassion. (1146) Beg for mercy for the whole world** (Diary 570). **No soul that has ever called upon my mercy has been disappointed** (Diary 1541).

Divine Mercy Sunday

Our Lord requested the feast and spoke these words to St. Faustina, "This feast emerged from the very depths of My mercy and it is confirmed in the vast depths of My tender mercies" (Diary 420). It is My desire that it be solemnly celebrated on the first Sunday after Easter. I desire that the feast of Mercy be refuge and shelter for all souls, and especially for poor sinners. On that day, the very depths of My tender mercy are open I pour out a whole ocean of graces upon those souls who approach the Fountain of My mercy" (Diary 699).

Responding affirmatively to our Lord's wishes, Pope John Paul II determined that the Roman Missal, after the title Second Sunday of Easter, there will be added Divine Mercy Sunday. *By virtue of Decree issued on May 5, 2000, by the Sacred Congregation for Divine Worship of Discipline of the Sacraments, the Holy See proclaimed the Second Sunday of Easter as Divine Mercy Sunday.*

Where the Second Sunday of Easter continues to proclaim in all its glory the Paschal Mystery of Christ: *His dying and rising and the glorious gift of new and everlasting life the new title, Divine Mercy Sunday adds the mystery of Divine Mercy. Divine Mercy Sunday is the climax of his revealing mercy and that Jesus is the true and living sign of inexhaustible mercy.* (John Paul II. Dives into Misericordia 8.7) With this new title we are lead to see clearly God's boundless mercy and love in all its goodness through his Son, Jesus Christ the Risen Lord. With great love the Lord gave us his only-begotten Son as our Redeemer – through his death and resurrection, He opens the door to eternal life for every human being. Divine Mercy shares with us the fullness of life, His image and leads us to the Mystery of His Divine Mercy.

In the Liturgy, the readings of the day focus on God the Father of our Lord *Jesus Christ, who in his great mercy gave us a new birth* (1Pt. 1:3) *and on the risen Savior who breathed on His disciples and bestowed on them the gift of the Holy Spirit, "Whose sins you forgive are forgiven them, and whose sins you retain are retained"* (Jn 20:20-23). The responsorial psalm over and over again calls us to praise and thank our Lord, "*For his mercy endures forever*" (Ps 118:2-4). Pope John Paul II describes it as the *"Sunday of Thanksgiving for all the goodness God has shown man in the entire Easter mystery"* (Regina Caeli Address, Divine Mercy Sunday, 1995).

Filled with love He comes to save us. The Feast of Divine Mercy Sunday is a commemoration of God's love and grace. He spoke this message to St. Faustina, "...My daughter, tell the whole world about My inconceivable mercy. I desire that the Feast of Mercy be a refuge and shelter for all souls, especially for poor sinners. On that day the very depths of My tender mercy are open. I pour out a whole ocean of graces upon those souls who approach the fount of My mercy. The soul that will go to Confession, and receive Holy Communion [on that day] shall obtain complete forgiveness of sins and punishment.

On that day all the divine floodgates through which graces flow are opened. Let no soul fear to draw near to Me, even though its sins be as scarlet. My mercy is so great that no mind, be it of man or of angel, will be able to fathom it throughout all eternity. Everything that exists has come forth from the very depths of My most tender mercy. Every soul in its relation to Me will contemplate My love and mercy throughout eternity.

The Feast of Mercy emerged from My very depths of tenderness. It is My desire that it be solemnly celebrated on the First Sunday after Easter. Mankind will not have peace until it turns to the Fount of My Mercy" (Diary 699).

Divine Mercy is not a new message but it helps us to again relive the Gospel of Easter more deeply. In this feast, He leads us to the paths of mercy which forgives sins and reaches out to all our needs. If we can learn of the Father's intense love and become one with Him, we will be able to look upon each other with kindness, forgiveness, solidarity. Mercy!

Jesus told St. Faustina, "On that day priests are to tell everyone about My great and unfathomable mercy" (Diary 570). Hardened sinners will repent on hearing their words...to priest who proclaim and extol My mercy I will give wondrous power; I will anoint their words and touch the hearts of those to whom they will speak" (Diary 1521).

Venerate the Divine Mercy image as Jesus said, "By means of this Image I shall be granting many graces to souls; so let every soul have access to it" (Diary 570).

You Are Not Yet Lost

On Good Friday in the year 1937 Jesus requested St. Faustina to make a special novena. He dictated the intentions for each day. She was directed to bring to His heart a different group of souls each day to be immersed in his ocean of mercy. The novena intentions are truly our Lord's intentions and we the Body of the Church are requested to be the intercessor at our Lord's side. Our Lord commanded St. Faustina write out the individual intentions for each day so this tells us he intends for us to pray the Divine Mercy Novena in preparation for Divine Mercy Sunday along with the Chaplet.

 Begin the Divine Mercy Novena on Good Friday.

 Recite the Chaplet along with the Novena Prayers for each day.

 Go to confession prior to Divine Mercy Sunday (the feast the Sunday after Easter) and sincerely repent all of your sins; say your very best confession.

 Receive Holy Communion on Divine Mercy Sunday.

 Put your complete TRUST in our Lord.

 Be kind and merciful to others through actions, words and deeds.

 Recite the chaplet.

 Venerate the Image of the Divine Mercy.

Celebrate Divine Mercy Sunday

Exposition
(following the Communion Prayer)

Hymn
> *O Salutaris*

Incensation

"At three o'clock, implore My mercy especially for sinners; and if only for a brief moment, immerse yourself in My Passion, particularly in My abandonment at the moment of agony. This is the hour of great mercy of the world. I will allow you to enter into My mortal sorrow. In this hour, I will refuse nothing to the soul that makes a request of me in virtue of My Passion" (Diary 1320).

"Ask of my faithful servant [priest] that, on this day, he tell the whole world of My great Mercy; that whoever approaches the Fount of Life on this day will be granted complete remission of sins and punishment.

Mankind will not have peace until it turns with trust to My mercy.

Oh, how much I am hurt by a soul's distrust! Such a soul professes that I am Holy and Just, but does not believe that I am Mercy and does not trust in My Goodness. Even the devils glorify My Justice but do not believe in My Goodness.

My Heart rejoices in this title of Mercy" (Diary 300).

As we meditate for a few moments on the passion of Jesus, consider it as if it had been undertaken for your sake alone.

Recite the Chaplet of the Divine Mercy (pg. 16-17).

"The Souls that say this chaplet will be embraced by My mercy during their lifetime and especially at the hour of their death."

The Blessing of the Image of the Divine Mercy
[Holy Water]

Leader:

    Lord you instructed St. Faustina to have an image painted according to Your pattern, promising it to be a vessel of Your grace and mercy. And when she complained to You that no one could paint You as beautiful as You are, You answered that Not in the beauty of color nor of the brush lies the sublimity of this image, but in My grace. We gather today to fulfill Your instructions to St. Faustina, to venerate Your image, to honor Your most generous Mercy, to pray for all mankind, to recite the Chaplet of Divine Mercy and to express our humble trust in You.

Leader:

    We pray for all mankind and especially all sinners: Most merciful Jesus, whose very nature it is to have compassion on us and to forgive us, do not look upon our sins but upon our trust which we place in Your infinite goodness. Receive us all into the abode of Your Most Compassionate Heart, and never let us escape from it. We beg this of You by Your love which unites You to the Father and the Holy Spirit.

Process with the Image

Benediction

Hymn
    Tantum Ergo

Holy Water/Incensation

Hymn
    Holy God We Praise Thy Name

Petitions of the Faithful

Leader:

Lord, You reminded us through St. Faustina's writings that every time we go to confession we are to immerse ourselves entirely in Your mercy with great trust for it is YOU, Lord, whom we approach in the Confessional. You are only hidden by the priest. Mindful of this, may our confessions always be very humble and sincere so we will profit from Your great grace, we pray…

All:

Jesus, we trust in You.

Leader:

Lord you remind us of the dreadful loathing you suffered in the Garden of Olives because of lukewarm souls. We must make every effort to be perfectly obedient to the Father's will and to grow in love and prayer, never allowing ourselves to become "lazy" in our response to Your love. May all lukewarm souls turn to Your Mercy for forgiveness and renewal we pray…

All:

Jesus, we trust in You.

Leader:

When souls are faced with seemingly insurmountable temptations, and are struggling with serious decisions, wanting to do what is right but afraid to make that decision, it is then Lord that we must have recourse to Your Divine Mercy. We must place ourselves completely in Your hands, asking You to help us overcome our fears and to guide us in the path You want us to take. For all souls who are facing such sufferings and for ourselves that we may come to their aid in prayer and deed we pray…

All:

Jesus, we trust in You.

Leader:

[Oh, if sinners knew My mercy they would not perish in such great numbers. Tell sinful souls not to be afraid to approach Me. On the cross the fountain of My mercy was opened wide by the lance for all souls - NO ONE WAS EXCLUDED.] Trust is the keystone. Help us Lord, for when we admit and reveal our sins, we are justly ashamed. But, we must remember that Your mercy is inexhaustible and that while not condoning the evil that was done, Your love for us is unwavering. All that is needed is to come to You, like the prodigal son. That we may heed Your calling and always turn to You, we pray…

All:

Jesus, we trust in You.

Leader:

Every time we say the "Our Father," help us to remember that when we say "forgive us as we forgive," what we are saying is forgive us in the same way we forgive those who trespass against us. Just as You are generous with your mercy, Jesus, we pray for the grace to be merciful to others. When someone comes to us and says, "please forgive me," it is easier to forgive. But, sadly, most people do not ask us to pardon them. More often, we receive the hurt, but not the request to forgive. It is then that the little word "as" takes on such meaning. To forgive silently in our hearts is to forgive as Jesus did. Remember how many times in the Gospels Jesus said "Your sins are forgiven." or "Father, forgive them." without being asked. Help us Lord.

All:

Jesus, we trust in You.

Leader:

[A reading may be read from a Gospel Book.]

Benediction

Veneration of the relic of St. Faustina Kowalska

Selection of Prayers

Conversion of Sinners

Jesus said to St. Faustina:

"You always console Me when you pray for sinners. The prayer most pleasing to Me is the prayer for their conversion. Know, My daughter, that this prayer is always heard and answered" (Diary 1397).

Jesus said to St. Faustina:

"I desire that you know more profoundly the love that burns in My Heart for souls, and you will understand this when you meditate upon My Passion. Call upon My mercy on behalf of sinners; desire their salvation. When you say this prayer with a contrite heart and with faith on behalf of some sinner, I will give him the grace of conversion. This is the prayer:

O Blood and Water, which gushed forth from the Heart of Jesus as a fountain of mercy for us, I trust in You" (Diary 186,187).

St. Faustina's Prayer for Sinners

O Jesus, eternal Truth, our Life, I call upon You and I beg Your mercy for poor sinners. O sweetest Heart of my Lord, full of pity and unfathomable mercy, I plead with You for poor sinners. O Most Sacred Heart, Fountain of Mercy from which gush forth rays of inconceivable graces upon the entire human race, I beg of You light for poor sinners. O Jesus, be mindful of your own bitter Passion and do not permit the loss of souls redeemed at so dear a price of Your most precious Blood. O Jesus, when I consider the great price for Your Blood, I rejoice at its immensity, for one drop alone would have been enough for the salvation of all sinners. Although sin is an abyss of wickedness and ingratitude, the price paid for us can never be equalled. Therefore, let every soul trust in the Passion of the Lord, and place its hope in His mercy. God will not deny His mercy to anyone. Heaven and earth may change, but God's mercy will never be exhausted. Oh, what immense joy burns in my heart when I contemplate Your incomprehensible goodness, O Jesus! I desire to bring all sinners to your feet that they may glorify Your mercy throughout endless ages (Diary 72).

In Times of Suffering

St. Faustina's Reflection:

If only the suffering soul knew how much God loves it, it would die of joy and excess of happiness! Someday, we will know the value of suffering, but then we will no longer be able to suffer. The present moment is ours (Diary 963).

Jesus, do not leave me alone in suffering. You know, Lord, how weak I am. I am an abyss of wretchedness, I am nothingness itself; so what will be so strange if You leave me alone and I fall? I am an infant, Lord, so I cannot get along by myself. However, beyond all abandonment, I trust, and in spite of my own feeling I trust, and I am being completely transformed into trust - often in spite of what I feel. Do not lessen any of my sufferings, only give me strength to bear them. Do with me as You please, Lord, only give me the grace to be able to love You in every event and circumstance. Lord, do not lessen my cup of bitterness, only give me strength that I may be able to drink it all (Diary 1489).

To the Mother of God

O Mary, my Mother and my Lady, I offer you my soul, my body, my life and my death, and all that will follow it. I place everything in your hands. O my Mother, cover my soul with your virginal mantle and grant me the grace of purity of heart, soul and body. Defend me with your power against all enemies, and especially against those who hide their malice behind the mask of virtue (Diary 79). *Fortify my soul that pain will not break it. Mother of grace, teach me to live by God's power* (Diary 315).

O Mary...a terrible sword has pierced your holy soul. Except for God, no one knows of your suffering. Your soul does not break; it is brave, because it is with Jesus, Sweet Mother, unite my soul to Jesus, because it is only then that I will be able to endure all trials and tribulations, and only in union with Jesus will my little sacrifices be pleasing to God. Sweetest Mother, continue to teach me about the interior life. May the sword of suffering never break me. O pure Virgin, pour courage into my heart and guard it (Diary 915).

For the Grace to Be Merciful to Others

This prayer gives us a true measure of our mercy, a mirror in which we observe ourselves as the merciful Christ. Make this your morning prayer and your evening examination of conscience.

O Most Holy Trinity! As many times as I breathe, as many times as my heart beats, as many times as my blood pulsates through my body, so many thousand times do I want to glorify Your mercy.

I want to be completely transformed into Your mercy and to be Your living reflection, O Lord. May the greatest of all divine attributes, that of Your unfathomable mercy, pass through my heart and soul to my neighbor.

Help me, O Lord that my eyes may be merciful, so that I may never suspect or judge from appearances, but look for what is beautiful in my neighbors' souls and come to their rescue.

Help me, that my ears may be merciful, so that I may give heed to my neighbors' needs and not be indifferent to their pains and moanings.

Help me, O Lord that my tongue may be merciful, so that I should never speak negatively of my neighbor, but have a word of comfort and forgiveness for all.

Help me, O Lord that my hands may be merciful and filled with good deeds, so that I may do only good to my neighbors and take upon myself the more difficult and toilsome tasks.

Help me, that my feet may be merciful, so that I may hurry to assist my neighbor, overcoming my own fatigue and weariness. My true rest is in the service of my neighbor.

Help me, O Lord that my heart may be merciful so that I myself may feel all the sufferings of my neighbor. I will refuse my heart to no one. I will be sincere even with those who I know will abuse my kindness. And I will lock myself up in the most merciful Heart of Jesus. I will bear my own suffering in silence. May Your mercy, O Lord, rest upon me.

You Yourself command me to exercise the three degrees of mercy. The first: the act of mercy of whatever kind. The second: the word of mercy – if I cannot carry out a work of mercy, I will assist by my words. The third: prayer – if I cannot show mercy by deeds or words, I can always do so by prayer. My prayer reaches out even there where I cannot reach out physically.

O my Jesus transform me into Yourself, for You can do all things (Diary 163).

The Memorare to St. Joseph

"Saint Joseph urged me to have a constant devotion to him. He himself told me to recite every day three prayers [the Our Father, Hail Mary and Glory Be], and the Memorare once every day. He has promised me his special help and protection. I recite the requested prayers every day and feel his special protection" (Diary 1203).

Remember, O most pure spouse of Mary, and my dearly beloved guardian, St. Joseph, that never was it known that anyone who invoked your care and requested your help was left without consolation. Inspired with this confidence, I come to you, and with all the ardor of my spirit I commend myself to you. Do not reject my prayer, O Foster Father of the Savior, but graciously receive and answer it. Amen.

For a Merciful Heart

O Jesus, I understand that Your mercy is beyond all imagining, and therefore I ask You to make my heart so big that there will be room in it for the needs of all the souls living on the face of the earth…and the souls suffering in Purgatory…make my heart sensitive to all the sufferings of my neighbor, whether of body or soul. O my Jesus, I know that You act toward us as we act toward our neighbor…make my heart like unto Your merciful Heart (692) *transform it into Your own Heart that I may sense the needs of other hearts, especially those who are sad and suffering. May the rays of mercy rest in my heart* (514)…*Jesus, help me to go through life doing good to everyone* (692).

For Priests

O my Jesus, I beg You on behalf of the whole Church: Grant it love and the light of Your Spirit and give power to the words of priests so that hardened hearts might be brought to repentance and return to You, O Lord. Lord, give us holy priests; You Yourself maintain them in holiness. O Divine and Great High Priest, may the power of Your mercy accompany them everywhere and protect them from the devil's traps and snares which are continually being set for the souls of priests. May the power of Your mercy, O Lord, shatter and bring to naught all that might tarnish the sanctity of priests, for You can do all things. I ask You for a special blessing and for light, O Jesus, for the priest before whom I will make confessions throughout my lifetime (Diary 240).

For One's Country
Most merciful Jesus, I beseech You through the intercession of Your Saints, and especially the intercession of Your dearest Mother who nurtured You from childhood; bless my native land. I beg You, Jesus, look not on our sins, but on the tears of little children, on the hunger and cold they suffer. Jesus, for the sake of these innocent ones, grant me the grace that I am asking of You for my country. (286) [The moment Saint Faustina said this prayer she saw Jesus, His eyes filled with tears; and He said to her: **"You see, my daughter, what great compassion I have for them. Know that it is they who uphold the world"** (Diary 286)].

For a Good Death
O merciful Jesus, stretched on the cross, be mindful of the hour of my death. O most merciful Heart of Jesus, opened with a lance, shelter me at the last moment of my life. O Blood and Water which gushed forth from the Heart of Jesus as a fountain of unfathomable mercy for me, O dying Jesus, Hostage of mercy, avert the Divine wrath at the hour of my death (Diary 813). *O my Jesus, may the last days of my exile be spent totally according to your most holy will. I unite my sufferings, my bitterness, and my last agony itself to your Sacred passion; and I offer myself for the whole world to obtain an abundance of God's mercy for souls. I firmly trust and commit myself entirely to Your holy will, which is mercy itself. Your mercy will be everything for me at the last hour* (Diary 1574).

For Divine Mercy
O Greatly Merciful God, Infinite Goodness, today all mankind calls from the abyss of its misery to Your mercy - to Your compassion, O God; and it is with its mighty voice of misery that it cries out: Gracious God, do not reject the prayer of this earths' exiles! O Lord, goodness beyond our understanding, Who are acquainted with our misery through and through and know that by our own power we cannot ascent to You, we implore You, anticipate us with Your grace and keep on increasing Your mercy in us, that we may faithfully do Your holy will all through our life and at death's hour. Let the omnipotence of Your mercy shield us form the darts of our salvation enemies, that we may with confidence, as Your children, await Your final coming - that day known to You alone. And we expect to obtain everything promised us by Jesus in spite of all our wretchedness. For Jesus is our Hope: Through His merciful Heart as through an open gate we pass through to heaven (Diary 1570).

"O blood and water, which gushed forth
from the heart of
Jesus, as a fount of mercy for us
I trust in You."
(Diary 187)

True Devotion

Private revelations and apparitions authenticated by the Church have added greatly to the devotion of Catholics. They remind us how we have not been paying attention to Jesus, the manifestation of divine will and truth. Calling us to turn away from sin and be faithful and to grow in the love of Jesus.

The Devotion to the Divine Mercy involves a total commitment to God as mercy. The practices of the devotion are completely in accordance with the teachings of the Church and are firmly rooted in the Gospel message of our Lord. The Divine Mercy Devotional leads us to the mystery of God's true mercy and love through our Redeemer and Savior, His son, Jesus Christ our Lord. When properly understood and enforced, this devotional will restore faith, nourish us and help us to grow as followers of Christ Jesus.

It is a reminder of what the Church has always taught us, that God is merciful and forgiving. We, too, must show mercy and forgiveness. The Divine Mercy Devotional takes us to a whole new center of interest, calling us to a profound understanding that God's love is unlimited and is available for every person, especially the most hardened sinners. The Divine Mercy Devotion is now the second most popular Catholic devotion in the world, surpassed only by the Holy Rosary.

I have grown to love and appreciate this devotion. I love that the Divine Mercy Chaplet unites us in two Sacraments, we receive the Mass and his mercy. I see the Divine Mercy devotion - praying and the Divine Mercy image - as a means the Lord established to help us adore and appreciate his mercy and love in the Sacrament of Confession.

I would encourage you to recite the Chaplet and to regularly pray the Divine Mercy Novena, to approach the Feast of Divine Mercy, and come to know the Lord more intimately through this ever-timely beautiful devotion.

www.ingramcontent.com/pod-product-compliance
Lightning Source LLC
Chambersburg PA
CBHW041812040426
42450CB00001B/11